THE HEALTHY KITCHEN

SUPERFOODS

hinkler

CONTENTS

Published by Hinkler Books Pty Ltd
45–55 Fairchild Street
Heatherton Victoria 3202 Australia
www.hinkler.com.au

Design © Hinkler Books Pty Ltd 2015
Food photography and recipe development
© Stockfood, The Food Media Agency
Typesetting: MPS Limited
Prepress: Graphic Print Group

ISBN: 978 1 7436 7733 9

Printed and bound in China

SUPERFOODS

Some foods are known as 'superfoods' because they're packed with nutrients necessary for health. Superfoods have been proven to help prevent cardiovascular disease, type 2 diabetes and certain cancers.

In this book, we have hand-picked 15 of the most common, accessible and versatile superfoods, and ensured at least one of them appears in every recipe. In most recipes there are two or more superfoods.

Chia seeds contain alpha-linolenic fatty acid. It is the only known essential omega-3 fatty acid the body can't produce. Try this superfood in our mouth-watering Banana and Chia Seed Puddings. **Sweet potatoes** are high in antioxidants, fibre, vitamins, manganese and potassium, while **quinoa** is gluten-free, high in B vitamins and potassium and a complete protein, because it contains all eight essential amino acids. The Sweet Potato and Cranberry Quinoa Cakes include both these superfoods.

Apples are a good source of vitamin C and contain important antioxidants; these fight the effects of harmful chemical changes in the body associated with ageing and also reduce the risk of heart disease and strokes. This fruit is also one of the best sources of pectin – a soluble fibre that binds to cholesterol, helping to lower cholesterol in the bloodstream.

Beetroot (beets) also contains soluble fibre, along with powerful antioxidants including betacyanin (which gives the vegetable its red colour), silica (which helps the body to utilise calcium), plus valuable minerals – potassium and iron – and vitamins A, B6 and C. The high concentration of nitrates in beetroot lowers blood pressure and helps prevent heart disease.

Pulses (legumes) such as **beans** and lentils are high in protein and a valuable source of vitamins and minerals – magnesium, copper and especially iron. They're also a useful source of folic acid, which is vital for normal tissue growth and essential for pregnant women in the first three months of pregnancy.

Berries such as **acai** are packed with antioxidants, amino acids and essential fatty acids. **Blueberries** contain compounds with an antioxidant capacity significantly higher than vitamins C or E.

Avocado – one of the most nutrient-dense foods – is incorporated into many meal recipes in this book, as well as delectable smoothies and a Chocolate and Avocado Mousse.

Broccoli, kale and **spinach** contain folic acid, potassium and chromium, which help regulate blood sugar and cholesterol levels. Broccoli also contains sulphoraphane, a phytochemical with anti-cancer properties.

Monounsaturated fat, which is good for the heart, is in **salmon** and olive oil, both rich in antioxidants. Salmon also contains omega-3 fatty acids, which lower cholesterol.

Other superfoods include **yoghurt,** a source of calcium useful for people who can't digest large amounts of lactose (milk sugar), and **eggs,** which provide protein, vitamins, iodine and phosphorus – essential for healthy bones and teeth.

Superfoods invigorate and nourish. These recipes combine ingredients with remarkable amounts of antioxidants, essential fatty acids, minerals, vitamins and phytonutrients. They'll make you feel as good as they taste!

BREAKFAST

For a refreshing start to the day, choose a breakfast that doesn't come out of a box. These creative recipes use wholesome ingredients that will give you a superfood energy boost.

ACAI BERRY BREAKFAST MOUSSE

Serves 4
Preparation and cooking 25 minutes + chilling 6 hours

Ingredients:

7 g | ¼ oz powdered gelatine
2 tbsp water
300 g | 11 oz acai puree
2 egg whites
4–5 tbsp honey
250 g | 9 oz | 1 cup thick Greek yoghurt, chilled
1 tsp vanilla extract

To serve:
muesli/granola (rolled oats, dried fruit, mixed nuts, bran flakes)
sliced bananas

Method:

1. Sprinkle the gelatine over the water and leave to stand for 5 minutes until spongy.

2. Heat the acai puree in a pan and bring to a boil. Reduce the heat and simmer for 5 minutes until thickened slightly. Cool for a few minutes.

3. Stir the gelatine into the puree. Set aside.

4. Whisk the egg whites until soft peaks form. Continue whisking while slowly drizzling in the honey. Continue whisking until stiff. Gradually fold the egg whites into the acai mixture.

5. Stir together the yoghurt and vanilla, then stir into the acai mixture.

6. Divide between 4 serving bowls, cover with cling wrap (plastic film) and chill for at least 6 hours until set.

7. Serve with muesli/granola and sliced bananas.

PERFECT POACHED-EGG BREAKFAST

Serves 4
Preparation and cooking 15 minutes

Ingredients:

4 eggs
100 g | 3½ oz spinach, washed
4 slices bread
butter
salt
freshly ground black pepper

Method:

1. Heat about 5 cm | 2" of water in a frying pan (skillet) to a simmer. Gently crack the eggs into a small bowl and slide them into the simmering water. Poach the eggs for 3–4 minutes, until just set.

2. Put the spinach in a pan with just the water clinging to the leaves, cover and bring to a boil. Cook for 1–2 minutes until wilted. Drain well.

3. Toast the bread and spread with the butter. Place on serving plates and place the spinach and eggs on top. Season to taste with salt and pepper.

BREAKFAST BURRITOS

Serves 4
Preparation and cooking 25 minutes

Ingredients:

2 tbsp olive oil
2 potatoes, diced
6 eggs
milk
salt
25 g | ¾ oz | ⅛ cup butter
pepper
spinach leaves
4 flour tortillas
3 tsp chopped parsley
100 g | 3½ oz | 1 cup grated cheddar (American) cheese

Method:

1. Heat the oil in a frying pan (skillet), add the potatoes and cook, stirring occasionally until golden and tender. Set aside.

2. Break the eggs into a pan and add the milk, salt and butter.

3. Cook over a medium heat, whisking all the time, until the eggs are scrambled. Season to taste with pepper.

4. Place a few spinach leaves on each tortilla.

5. Spoon a layer of potatoes and scrambled eggs down the centre of each tortilla. Sprinkle with parsley.

6. Top with the cheese, then fold over the edges of the tortillas and roll up.

Tip: To reheat the burritos, wrap in foil and place in a warm oven for a few minutes until heated through.

ELDERBERRY AND APPLE BLINIS

Serves 4
Preparation and cooking 40 minutes

Ingredients:

100 g | 3½ oz | 1 cup (scant) self-raising wholemeal (wholewheat) flour
50 g | 1¾ oz | ½ cup rolled oats
½ tsp bicarbonate of (baking) soda
1 tsp ground cinnamon
1 pinch salt
1 large egg
200 ml | 7 fl oz | ⅞ cup buttermilk
2 tbsp sunflower oil
1 tbsp water
2 small eating apples, unpeeled and grated
4 tbsp elderberries (or blueberries, if preferred)

For the caramelised apples:
55 g | 2 oz | ¼ cup butter
4 eating apples, peeled and diced
4 tbsp caster (superfine) sugar
2 tsp ground cinnamon

To serve:
icing (confectioner's) sugar
honey
yoghurt

Method:

1. Combine the flour, oats, bicarbonate of (baking) soda, cinnamon and salt in a mixing bowl.

2. Whisk together the egg, buttermilk, 1 tablespoon of oil and the water. Stir in the grated apples and elderberries.

3. Stir the buttermilk mixture into the dry ingredients to make a thick batter.

4. Heat a little oil in a heavy frying pan (skillet).

5. Spoon about 2 tablespoons of the batter into the hot pan. Cook for 3–4 minutes until bubbles start to appear on the surface of each blini, then turn over and gently cook on the other side for another 3–4 minutes, until the blinis are cooked through.

6. Repeat until all the batter is used, layering the blinis with non-stick baking paper until required.

7. For the caramelised apples: heat the butter in a frying pan and add the apples, sugar and cinnamon. Cook over a medium heat for about 10 minutes, turning occasionally until evenly caramelised.

8. Layer the blinis with the caramelised apples. Sift icing (confectioner's) sugar over the top and drizzle with honey. Serve with yoghurt.

Tip: Do not eat raw elderberries. They must be cooked to be edible.

BLUEBERRY OAT MUFFINS

Makes 12 muffins
Preparation and cooking 45 minutes

Ingredients:

110 g | 4 oz | ¾ cup wholemeal (wholewheat) flour
75 g | 2½ oz | ¾ cup plain (all-purpose) flour
1½ tsp baking powder
½ tsp bicarbonate of (baking) soda
100 g | 3½ oz | 1 cup rolled oats, plus extra for sprinkling
75 g | 2½ oz | ⅓ cup caster (superfine) sugar
2 eggs
2 tbsp clear honey
170 ml | 6 fl oz | ¾ cup buttermilk
55 ml | 2 fl oz | 11 tsp sunflower oil
1 tsp vanilla extract
125 g | 4½ oz | 1 cup blueberries

Method:

1. Heat the oven to 200°C (180°C fan | 400°F | gas 6). Line a 12-hole muffin tin with paper cases.

2. Sift together both flours, baking powder and bicarbonate of (baking) soda into a mixing bowl. Stir in the rolled oats and sugar.

3. Whisk together the eggs and honey until smooth. Add the buttermilk, oil and vanilla and whisk until blended.

4. Add to the flour mixture and mix until only just combined. The mixture will be lumpy. Fold in the blueberries.

5. Spoon into the paper cases and sprinkle lightly with oats.

6. Bake for 20–25 minutes, until risen and golden. Cool in the tins for 5 minutes, then place on a wire rack to cool completely.

BREAKFAST FRY

Serves 4
Preparation and cooking 35 minutes

Ingredients:

350 g | 12 oz new potatoes, sliced
salt
3 tbsp butter
1 onion, chopped
100 g | 3½ oz button mushrooms, halved
freshly ground black pepper
300 g | 11 oz spinach, chopped
4 eggs
½ tsp chilli (red pepper) flakes

Method:

1. Cook the potatoes in a pan of boiling salted water for about 5 minutes until just tender. Drain well.

2. Heat 2 tablespoons of butter in a frying pan (skillet) and cook the onion and mushrooms for 8–10 minutes until softened.

3. Add the potatoes and season with salt and pepper. Cook for a few minutes until the potatoes are golden.

4. Add the spinach and remaining butter and cook, stirring, until the butter has melted.

5. Make 4 wells in the mixture and break an egg into each well. Reduce the heat, cover and cook for 5–6 minutes until the eggs are set. Sprinkle with chilli (red pepper) flakes and serve immediately.

POTATO PANCAKES WITH SCRAMBLED EGGS

Makes 12–14 pancakes
Preparation and cooking 25 minutes

Ingredients:

3 large potatoes, grated
1 egg, beaten
80 g | 3 oz | ¾ cup plain (all-purpose) flour, more if needed
40 g | 1½ oz | ¼ cup polenta (cornmeal)
1½ tsp baking powder
½ tsp salt
freshly ground pepper
vegetable oil, for frying

For the scrambled eggs:
25 g | 1 oz | ⅛ cup butter
1 green capsicum (pepper), seeds removed, chopped
1 onion, chopped
4 large eggs
3–4 tbsp milk
1 pinch salt
freshly ground pepper
snipped chives

To serve:
smoked salmon
crème fraîche
tomato sauce

Method:

1. Mix the potatoes, egg, flour, polenta (cornmeal), baking powder, salt and pepper to a thick batter. If it is too thin add a little more flour.

2. Heat the oil in a frying pan (skillet) to a depth of about 1 cm | ½" until hot.

3. Drop spoonfuls of the potato mixture into the hot oil, a few at a time; reduce the heat and cook for about 5 minutes on each side, until crisp and golden. Drain on absorbent kitchen paper.

4. Heat the butter in a shallow pan and cook the capsicum (pepper) and onions until soft, but not browned.

5. Beat together the eggs, milk and salt and stir into the pan.

6. Stir over a low heat until the scrambled eggs are cooked through, but still light and fluffy. Season with salt and pepper and add the chives.

7. Layer the pancakes with scrambled eggs. Top with smoked salmon and crème fraîche and serve with tomato sauce.

BREAKFAST QUINOA

Serves 4
Preparation and cooking 25 minutes

Ingredients:

170 g | 6 oz | 1 cup quinoa
450 ml | 16 fl oz | 2 cups water
75 g | 2½ oz | 1 cup chopped almonds
2–3 tbsp maple syrup
225 g | 8 oz | 1 cup Greek yoghurt
100 g | 3½ oz | 1 cup blueberries
125 g | 4½ oz | 1 cup raspberries
ground cinnamon

Method:

1. Put the quinoa and water into a pan. Cover and bring to a boil.

2. Reduce the heat to low and simmer for 15 minutes. Remove from the heat and leave to stand for 5 minutes.

3. Stir in the almonds and maple syrup to taste. Fluff with a fork and set aside to cool.

4. Divide between 4 serving bowls and top with the yoghurt and berries. Sprinkle with a little cinnamon.

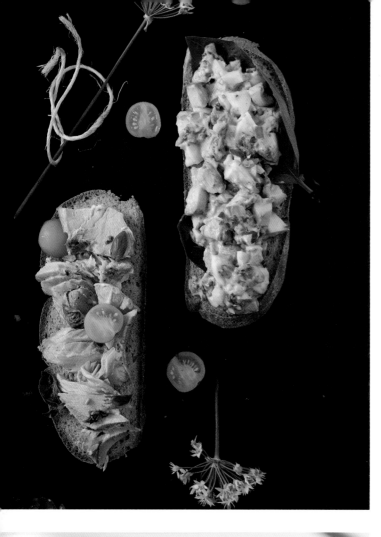

LUNCH

These healthy lunch recipes are a great way to increase your superfood intake. There are hearty lunches for the cooler months, lighter lunches for the warmer months and options that work well all year round.

KALE AND PASTA SALAD

Serves 4
Preparation and cooking 25 minutes

Ingredients:

225 g | 8 oz wholemeal (wholewheat) pasta
1 tsp salt
water
225 g | 8 oz kale leaves, coarsely chopped
225 g | 8 oz blue cheese, crumbled
freshly ground black pepper

For the dressing:
1 tbsp lemon juice
2 tbsp cider or white wine vinegar
2–3 tbsp red pesto
2 tbsp extra virgin olive oil

Method:

1. Cook the pasta in a pan of boiling salted water according to the packet instructions, and drain.

2. For the dressing: mix together the lemon juice, vinegar and pesto, then whisk in the olive oil until smooth.

3. Gently stir into the warm pasta, then add the kale and cheese. Season to taste with pepper and toss well.

BROWN RICE SALMON SUSHI

Makes 30–40 pieces
Preparation and cooking 1 hour 10 minutes + standing 15 minutes

Ingredients:

250 g | 9 oz | 1⅛ cups brown sushi rice
salt
2 tbsp rice wine or rice vinegar
5 sheets nori sushi
3 tsp wasabi paste
350 g | 12 oz sashimi-quality salmon, diced
1 avocado, thinly sliced and chopped

Method:

1. Cook the rice in a pan of boiling salted water according to the directions on the pack.

2. Tip the rice onto a large flat tray. Add the rice wine and toss the rice, turning frequently, and leave to cool to room temperature.

3. Put a sheet of nori sushi on your work surface. With dampened fingers, spread ⅕ of the rice over the seaweed, about ½ cm | ⅕" thick. Flatten down then carefully flip the nori sushi onto a plastic-covered bamboo sushi mat, rice side down. Leave the quarter the furthest away from you plain.

4. Smear a little wasabi in a line a little off-centre on the side of the nori nearest to you. Follow with a layer of salmon, then avocado down the centre. Roll up the bamboo mat slowly, pressing lightly with both hands. Remove the roll from the mat and set aside to stand with the joining edges underneath. Repeat the process with the remaining seaweed sheets, wasabi, rice, salmon and avocado.

5. Cover each roll with cling wrap (plastic film). Trim the ends with a lightly moistened sharp knife and cut each roll into 6–8 pieces. Remove the plastic. Serve immediately.

Tip: If you can't find brown sushi rice, use round-grain brown rice instead.

SUPERFOOD SANDWICHES

Serves 4
Preparation and cooking 25 minutes

Ingredients:

For the avocado sandwich:
2 hard-boiled eggs, chopped
2 small avocados, pitted and diced
1 tbsp plain Greek yoghurt
1 tbsp lemon juice
2 spring (green) onions, chopped
¼ tsp dijon mustard
salt
freshly ground black pepper
baby spinach leaves
2–3 slices wholemeal (wholewheat) bread

For the salmon sandwich:
4 tbsp plain Greek yoghurt
4 tsp lemon juice
2 tsp snipped chives
salt
freshly ground black pepper
100 g | 3½ oz poached or steamed skinless salmon fillet,
    flaked into chunks
2–3 slices wholemeal bread
basil leaves
yellow cherry tomatoes, halved

Method:

1. For the avocado sandwich: mix the hard-boiled eggs, avocado, yoghurt, lemon juice, spring (green) onions and mustard until well combined. Season to taste with salt and pepper.

2. Arrange the spinach leaves on the bread and top with the avocado mixture. Serve immediately.

3. For the salmon sandwich: mix together the yoghurt, lemon juice and chives, and season with salt and pepper in a small bowl.

4. Gently stir the salmon into the dressing.

5. Arrange on the bread slices, sprinkle with black pepper and garnish with basil. Arrange the cherry tomatoes on the bread and serve immediately.

QUINOA AND SWEET POTATO SALAD

Serves 4
Preparation and cooking 25 minutes

Ingredients:

200 g | 7 oz | 1 cup (heaped) quinoa
4 tbsp olive oil
4 sweet potatoes (yams), peeled and cubed
200 g | 7 oz fetta cheese, crumbled
2 handfuls baby spinach

For the dressing:
100 ml | 3½ fl oz | 7 tbsp extra virgin olive oil
2 tbsp cider vinegar
2 tsp honey
salt and pepper

Method:

1. Cook the quinoa according to the packet instructions. Drain, rinse and set aside.

2. Heat the oil in a pan and gently cook the sweet potatoes (yams), stirring from time to time, for about 8 minutes until tender.

3. For the dressing: whisk together the oil, vinegar and honey and season to taste.

4. Combine the salad ingredients, toss with the dressing and serve.

VEGETABLE FRITTATA

Serves 4
Preparation and cooking 25 minutes

Ingredients:

1 tbsp olive oil
1 onion, chopped
2 sweet potatoes (yams), peeled and coarsely grated
1 clove garlic, crushed
2 tsp chopped thyme leaves
225 g | 8 oz broccoli, cut into small florets (flowerets)
salt
4 firm tomatoes, roughly chopped
75 g | 2½ oz fetta cheese, diced
7 eggs
3 tbsp water
salt
freshly ground pepper

To serve:
asparagus

Method:

1. Heat the olive oil in a frying pan (skillet) and cook the onion for 2 minutes. Add the sweet potatoes (yams) and cook, stirring, for a further 5 minutes, until softened. Stir in the garlic and thyme and cook for 1 minute.

2. Cook the broccoli in a pan of boiling salted water for 3 minutes, until al dente. Drain and stir into the potato mixture with the tomatoes and fetta.

3. Heat the grill (broiler).

4. Beat the eggs with the water, season to taste and pour into the pan. Reduce the heat and cook for 10–15 minutes until the frittata is almost set.

5. Place the pan under the hot grill for 2–3 minutes, until golden and set.

6. Cut into slices and serve with asparagus.

VEGETABLE SOUP

Serves 4
Preparation and cooking 2 hours

Ingredients:

200 g | 7 oz | 1 cup dried white beans, soaked overnight
200 g | 7 oz | 1 cup dried black beans, soaked overnight
2 tbsp olive oil
1 onion, chopped
1 clove garlic, chopped
200 g | 7 oz carrots, chopped
1 stick celery, chopped
1 potato, peeled and diced
250 g | 9 oz kale, chopped
500 ml | 18 fl oz | 2 cups vegetable stock (broth)
300 g | 11 oz ripe tomatoes, quartered
salt and pepper
225 g | 8 oz salsiccia (Italian sausage), sliced

To garnish:
grated parmesan cheese
curly kale

Method:

1. Rinse all the beans and put into a pan with fresh water to cover. Bring to a boil and cook for about 45 minutes until tender.

2. Drain, then mash ¾ of the beans.

3. Heat the oil in a large heavy-based pan and gently cook the onion and garlic until translucent.

4. Add the carrots, celery, potato and kale and cook for a few minutes.

5. Pour in the stock (broth) and add the mashed beans. Simmer gently for 25 minutes.

6. Add the tomatoes and remaining beans and season with salt and pepper. Simmer for a further 10–15 minutes.

7. Heat a little oil in a frying pan (skillet) and fry the salsiccia (Italian sausage) until crisp.

8. Place a steamer insert into a pan and fill with water to just below the bottom of the steamer. Cover and bring the water to a boil over high heat. Add the kale and steam for 7–10 minutes until just tender.

9. Pour the soup into warmed serving bowls and divide the salsiccia between the bowls.

10. Sprinkle with parmesan cheese and garnish with curly kale.

FRESH BEETROOT SALAD

Serves 4
Preparation and cooking 40 minutes + cooling 30 minutes

Ingredients:

4 medium beetroots (beets)
3 potatoes
4 carrots
1 small onion, finely chopped
3 gherkins (dill pickles), chopped
400 g | 14 oz canned butter (lima) beans, drained
3–4 tbsp mayonnaise
salt

To garnish:
dill (dill weed)

Method:

1. Cook the whole unpeeled beetroots (beets), potatoes and carrots in separate pans of boiling water for about 25 minutes until tender. Drain and cover with chilled water. Set aside to cool.

2. When the vegetables are cool, remove from water, peel and dice into small cubes.

3. Mix together the vegetables, onion, gherkin (pickles) and beans until combined. Stir in the mayonnaise and season with salt.

4. Put into a serving dish and garnish with dill (dill weed). Serve immediately.

SWEET POTATO AND CRANBERRY QUINOA CAKES

Serves 4–6
Preparation and cooking 1 hour 30 minutes + standing 15 minutes

Ingredients:

85 g | 3 oz | ½ cup wild rice, well rinsed
salt
1 tbsp olive oil
1 onion, finely chopped
2 cloves garlic, crushed
330 g | 12 oz | 1¾ cups quinoa
675 ml | 24 fl oz | 3 cups water
1 tsp paprika
2 cooked sweet potatoes (yams), mashed
2 eggs, beaten
25 g | 1 oz | ½ cup wholemeal (wholewheat) breadcrumbs
75 g | 2½ oz | ½ cup dried cranberries
pepper

Method:

1. Cook the wild rice in a pan of boiling salted water according to the directions on the pack. Drain well and set aside.

2. Heat the olive oil in a large pan and cook the onion and garlic until softened.

3. Add the quinoa, water and paprika. Cover, bring to a boil and then reduce the heat and simmer for 10–15 minutes until the liquid is absorbed. Tip into a bowl.

4. Add the sweet potato (yam) and mix well, then add the wild rice, eggs, breadcrumbs and cranberries and stir until thoroughly combined. Season to taste with salt and pepper.

5. Leave to stand for 15 minutes.

6. Heat the oven to 200°C (180°C fan | 400°F | gas 6). Line a large baking tray (sheet) with non-stick baking paper.

7. Shape the cooled mixture into patties and place on the baking tray.

8. Bake for 20–25 minutes until golden and piping hot. Cool on the tray for 5 minutes before serving.

DINNER

Try these recipes for healthy dinners that are full of colour, flavour and nutritious superfoods. They are easy to prepare for everyday dinners but impressive enough for entertaining.

WHOLEMEAL QUICHE WITH SALMON

Serves 4–6
Preparation and cooking 1 hour 35 minutes + chilling 30 minutes

Ingredients:

For the pastry:
115 g | 4 oz | 1 cup plain (all-purpose) flour, plus extra
   for dusting
115 g | 4 oz | 1 cup wholemeal (wholewheat) flour
1 pinch salt
25 g | 1 oz | ⅛ cup copha (vegetable shortening)
1 egg yolk, beaten
2 tbsp water

For the filling:
400 g | 14 oz salmon fillet
1 tbsp olive oil
salt and pepper
4 eggs
400 ml | 14 fl oz | 1⅔ cups double (heavy, 48% fat) cream
2 tbsp chopped dill (dill weed)

To garnish:
broccoli, broken into florets (flowerets)
dried cranberries
1 dill flower

Method:

1. For the pastry: sift the flour into a mixing bowl and stir in the salt. Rub in the copha (shortening) until the mixture resembles breadcrumbs. Stir in the egg yolk and water, until the mixture just comes together. Roll the dough into a ball, then wrap in cling wrap (plastic film) and chill for 30 minutes.

2. Heat the oven to 190°C (170°C fan | 375°F | gas 5). Lightly grease a deep 23 cm | 9" flan dish or tin.

3. Roll out the pastry on a floured surface and line the tin. Prick the pastry all over with a fork, line the pastry case with non-stick baking paper and fill with rice or dried beans. Bake for 15 minutes. Remove the paper and beans and bake for a further 8–10 minutes until golden and cooked through.

4. Reduce the oven temperature to 180°C (160°C fan | 350°F | gas 4).

5. For the filling: Put the salmon in a baking dish, brush with oil, season lightly with salt and pepper and bake for 10–15 minutes, until the fish flakes easily. Remove from the oven and leave to cool slightly.

6. Break the salmon into large pieces and place in the pastry case.

7. Whisk together the eggs and cream and stir in the dill (dill weed). Pour into the pastry case.

8. Bake for 20–25 minutes, until the filling is set and golden.

9. Put the broccoli florets (flowerets) into a steamer or colander, set over a pan of boiling water. Cover with a lid or tight-fitting foil and steam for 5 minutes.

10. Garnish the quiche with steamed broccoli, dried cranberries and dill flower.

HEALTHY BEAN BURGERS

Makes 4 burgers
Preparation and cooking 30 minutes + chilling 1 hour

Ingredients:

6 tbsp olive oil
1 carrot, finely chopped
1 onion, finely chopped
1 clove garlic, finely chopped
100 g | 3½ oz | 2 cups wholemeal (wholewheat) breadcrumbs
2 tsp mild chilli powder
2 tbsp tomato sauce (ketchup)
1 egg, beaten
400 g | 14 oz canned red kidney beans, rinsed and drained
salt and pepper

To serve:
1–2 tbsp vegetable oil
4 eggs
4 crusty rolls
shredded lettuce
8 slices tomato

Method:

1. Heat half the oil in a frying pan (skillet) and gently cook the carrot, onion and garlic for about 5 minutes, until softened. Tip into a bowl.

2. Add the breadcrumbs, chilli powder, tomato sauce (ketchup) and egg and mix well to blend. Add the kidney beans and roughly mash together. Season to taste with salt and pepper and leave to cool a little.

3. Shape into patties and chill for 1 hour.

4. Heat the remaining oil in a frying pan and cook the burgers for 3–4 minutes on each side until golden.

5. To serve: heat the oil in a frying pan and crack in the eggs. Baste the yolks with hot oil and fry until cooked to your liking.

6. Split open the rolls and put the lettuce and tomatoes on the bases, then place the burgers on top. Add a fried egg and replace the tops of the rolls.

SWEET POTATO LASAGNE

Serves 6
Preparation and cooking 1 hour 30 minutes

Ingredients:

900 g | 32 oz sweet potatoes (yams), sliced
225 g | 8 oz carrots, sliced
2 zucchinis (courgettes), chopped
4 firm tomatoes, chopped
3 tbsp olive oil
1 tsp salt
8 sheets lasagne

For the sauce:
3 tbsp olive oil
25 g | 1 oz | ¼ cup plain (all-purpose) flour
1 l | 35 fl oz | 4 cups hot milk
salt
freshly ground pepper
1 pinch grated nutmeg
1 pinch cayenne (red) pepper
200 g | 7 oz | 2 cups grated mozzarella cheese
50 g | 1¾ oz | ½ cup grated parmesan cheese

To garnish:
basil

Method:

1. Heat the oven to 200°C (180°C fan | 400°F | gas 6).

2. Put all the vegetables in a roasting tin and add the oil and salt. Toss well together until the vegetables are coated in oil. Cook for about 30 minutes until tender. Remove from the oven and set aside.

3. Cook the lasagne sheets in a pan of boiling salted water for 3 minutes, then drain well.

4. Reduce the oven temperature to 180°C (160°C fan | 350°F | gas 4). Grease a large baking dish.

5. For the sauce: heat the oil in a pan and whisk in the flour. Cook gently, without browning, for 2–3 minutes. Whisk in the hot milk and bring to a boil, stirring until mixture thickens. Season with salt, pepper, nutmeg and cayenne (red) pepper to taste.

6. Spoon about 125 ml | ½ cup of sauce into the baking dish. Cover with a layer of lasagne sheets, then a layer of vegetables. Spread with 375 ml | 1½ cups sauce and half the grated mozzarella. Repeat the layers. Sprinkle with parmesan.

7. Bake for 25–30 minutes, until bubbling and browned on top. Rest for 10 minutes before serving.

8. Garnish with basil.

SUPERFOOD SALAD

Serves 4
Preparation and cooking 1 hour 45 minutes

Ingredients:

3 red onions
6 medium beetroots (beets)
2 large sweet potatoes (yams)
6 cloves garlic
2–3 tbsp olive oil
150 g | 5 oz baby spinach leaves
2 tbsp extra virgin olive oil
1 tbsp red wine vinegar
2 tsp finely chopped thyme
salt
freshly ground black pepper
125 g | 4½ oz creamy fetta cheese

Method:

1. Heat the oven to 180°C (160°C fan | 350°F | gas 4).

2. Coat the vegetables and garlic with olive oil and put into a roasting tin. Cook the onions, sweet potatoes (yams) and garlic for about 1 hour until tender – the beetroot (beets) will need about 20 minutes longer. Set aside to cool.

3. Peel the vegetables and cut into pieces the same size.

4. Arrange the spinach leaves on a serving plate. Place the vegetables and garlic over the spinach.

5. Whisk together the extra virgin olive oil, vinegar and thyme and season with salt and pepper. Drizzle over the salad and crumble the cheese over the top. Serve immediately.

BEAN STEW WITH MEATBALLS

Serves 4
Preparation and cooking 1 hour 50 minutes

Ingredients:

For the stew:

250 g | 9 oz | 1¼ cups dried cannellini (navy) beans, soaked overnight

2 tbsp olive oil

1 onion, chopped

2 carrots, diced

1 stick celery, diced

2 cloves garlic, finely chopped

400 g | 14 oz canned chopped tomatoes

200 ml | 7 fl oz | ⅞ cup vegetable stock (broth)

7 tbsp red wine

salt and pepper

1 bouquet garni, fresh or dried

For the meatballs:

500 g | 18 oz minced (ground) beef

1 egg

50 g | 1¾ oz | 1 cup breadcrumbs

1 tbsp finely chopped parsley

salt and pepper

2 tbsp olive oil

To garnish:

flat-leaf parsley

Method:

1. For the stew: put the drained beans in a large pan and bring to a boil. Boil briskly for 10 minutes and drain.

2. Heat the oil in a frying pan (skillet) and fry the onion for 5 minutes until softened. Add the carrots, celery and garlic and cook for 2 minutes.

3. Add the tomatoes, stock (broth), wine, salt and pepper and bring to a boil.

4. Stir the hot tomato mixture into the beans and bring to a boil.

5. For the meatballs: mix the beef with the egg, breadcrumbs and parsley. Season with salt and pepper and form into balls about the size of a walnut.

6. Heat the oil in a frying pan and fry the meatballs until browned on all sides.

7. Put into the bean stew with the bouquet garni, cover and cook for about 1 hour until the beans are tender.

8. Garnish with flat-leaf parsley.

Tip: A bouquet garni is a bundle of herbs, such as bay leaves, parsley and thyme, tied together with string. Dried bouquet garni can also be found at most supermarkets.

SPAGHETTI WITH SALMON, ASPARAGUS AND BROAD BEANS

Serves 4
Preparation and cooking 40 minutes

Ingredients:

1 tbsp olive oil
6 spring (green) onions, chopped
6 tbsp dry white wine
200 g | 7 oz | ⅞ cup crème fraîche
salt
freshly ground pepper
grated nutmeg
½ small lemon, juice
175 g | 6 oz young broad (fava) beans
350 g | 12 oz spaghetti
175 g | 6 oz asparagus, cut into short lengths
100 g | 3½ oz smoked salmon, cut into small pieces

Method:

1. Heat the oil in a pan and cook the spring (green) onions for 1 minute, until softened.

2. Add the wine and boil vigorously until reduced to about 2 tablespoons.

3. Stir in the crème fraîche, season well and add the nutmeg. Bring to a boil and simmer for 2–3 minutes until slightly thickened. Stir in the lemon juice. Set aside.

4. Blanch the shelled broad (fava) beans in a pan of boiling salted water for 2–3 minutes. Drain and rinse under cold running water. Peel off the outer hard skin.

5. Cook the spaghetti in a pan of salted boiling water, according to the packet directions, adding the asparagus 3 minutes before the end of cooking time. Drain well, reserving a little pasta water.

6. Toss the hot spaghetti and asparagus with the drained broad beans, smoked salmon and sauce, adding a little pasta water. Stir over a gentle heat to warm through. Serve immediately.

LAMB CURRY

Serves 4
Preparation and cooking 1 hour 30 minutes

Ingredients:

3 cloves garlic
thumb-size piece ginger (gingerroot), peeled and roughly chopped
2 green chillis, seeds removed and roughly chopped
1 onion, roughly chopped
125 ml | 4½ fl oz | ½ cup vegetable oil
800 g | 28 oz lamb shoulder, cut into large chunks
2 tsp coriander seeds, crushed
2 cardamom pods, crushed
1 tsp cumin seeds, crushed
1 tsp garam masala
1 tsp turmeric
1 tsp salt
1 tbsp tomato paste (puree)
250 ml | 9 fl oz | 1 cup lamb stock (broth) or water
2 large handfuls spinach, washed and roughly chopped

Method:

1. Put the garlic, ginger (gingerroot), chillis and onion in a food processor and blend to make a puree. Set aside.

2. Heat the oil in a wide pan and brown the meat pieces on all sides. Remove the meat from the pan and set aside.

3. Fry the spices in the oil for 2 minutes then add the salt and onion puree and cook for 3 minutes.

4. Return the meat to the pan, add the tomato paste (puree) and lamb stock (broth), then cover and simmer very gently for about 45 minutes. Add a little water during the cooking if needed.

5. Add the spinach to the pan and cook for a further 30 minutes or until the lamb is very tender.

CHICKEN STEW WITH COUSCOUS

Serves 4
Preparation and cooking 1 hour

Ingredients:

1 tbsp olive oil
1 onion, chopped
1 clove garlic, finely chopped
½ tsp ground cumin
½ tsp ground coriander
1 tbsp tomato paste (puree)
800 g | 28 oz canned chopped tomatoes
200 ml | 7 fl oz | ⅞ cup water
750 g | 26 oz butternut pumpkin (squash), seeds removed and chopped
500 g | 18 oz boneless chicken breast, diced
150 g | 5 oz baby spinach
200 g | 7 oz | 1 cup (heaped) couscous
75 g | 2½ oz | ½ cup dried apricots, roughly chopped
50 g | 1¾ oz | ⅓ cup raisins
275 ml | 10 fl oz | 1⅛ cups boiling water
salt
freshly ground black pepper

Method:

1. Heat the oil in a pan and cook the onion for 5–10 minutes until softened. Add the garlic and spices and cook for 1 minute.

2. Stir in the tomato paste (puree), chopped tomatoes and water and bring to a boil.

3. Add the butternut pumpkin (squash), cover and cook for 20 minutes.

4. Add the chicken and cook for a further 10–15 minutes until the chicken is cooked through. Just before serving stir through the spinach until just wilted.

5. Place the couscous, apricots and raisins in a bowl and pour over the boiling water. Cover and leave to stand for 10 minutes until all the water has been absorbed.

6. Fluff with a fork and season to taste with salt and pepper.

7. Serve the couscous with the chicken stew.

DESSERT

Following a healthy eating plan doesn't mean you have to deny yourself dessert. These delicious dessert recipes include plenty of superfoods so you can still enjoy some sweetness in your life.

MASCARPONE CAKE

Serves 4–6

Preparation and cooking 30 minutes + standing 15 minutes + chilling 12 hours

Ingredients:

For the base:
150 g | 5 oz | 1½ cups oat biscuit crumbs
55 g | 2 oz | ¼ cup unsalted butter, melted

For the filling:
3 eggs, separated
125 g | 4½ oz | ½ cup caster (superfine) sugar
1 unwaxed lemon, finely grated zest
750 g | 26 oz | 3⅓ cups low-fat cream cheese (quark)
6 leaves gelatine, cut into strips
3 tbsp hot water

To decorate:
raspberries
blueberries
blackberries
icing (confectioner's) sugar
white crisped-rice chocolate bars, cut into pieces

Method:

1. For the base: Butter a 20 cm | 8" springform tin. Stir together the biscuit crumbs and melted butter. Press into the base of the tin and chill.

2. For the filling: whisk together the egg yolks, sugar and lemon zest until thick and pale.

3. Add the low-fat cream cheese (quark) and whisk until smooth. Leave to stand for 15 minutes.

4. Soak the gelatine in 2–3 tablespoons of cold water in a small bowl or cup for 5 minutes.

5. Pour over the hot water and stir until the gelatine has dissolved.

6. Whisk the cream cheese mixture and gradually stir in 3 tablespoons of the gelatine. Gradually stir all the gelatine into the cream cheese mixture.

7. Whisk the egg whites until stiff and gradually fold into the cream cheese mixture.

8. Carefully pour onto the base and smooth the surface. Cover and chill overnight.

9. Place the cake on a serving plate and decorate the top with berries. Sift icing (confectioner's) sugar over the top. Arrange the crisped-rice chocolate bars around the sides of the cake.

CHOCOLATE AND AVOCADO MOUSSE

Serves 4–6
Preparation and cooking 20 minutes + chilling 2 hours

Ingredients:

80 g | 3 oz | 11 tsp honey
2 ripe avocados, peeled
1 tsp vanilla extract
55 g | 2 oz | ½ cup raw cacao powder
1 pinch salt
1 pinch ground cinnamon
2 tbsp coconut oil, melted

To serve:
raspberries
cacao powder

Method:

1. Put all the ingredients into a blender or food processor and blend until smooth and creamy.

2. Spoon into serving glasses and chill for about 2 hours until set.

3. Top with raspberries and sift a little cacao powder over the top before serving.

BLUEBERRY ICE-CREAM

Serves 4–6
Preparation and cooking 25 minutes + freezing 4 hours

Ingredients:

100 g | 3½ oz | 1 cup blueberries
80 g | 3 oz | ¾ cup icing (confectioner's) sugar
600 ml | 21 fl oz | 2½ cups double (heavy, 48% fat) cream
2 tsp vanilla extract
8 oat biscuits (cookies), roughly crushed

Method:

1. Heat the blueberries and 4 tablespoons icing (confectioner's) sugar in a pan and bring to a simmer, stirring. Simmer gently for about 5 minutes, then set aside to cool.

2. Whisk the cream until soft peaks form. Sift in the remaining icing sugar, add the vanilla and whisk until thick.

3. Add the biscuit crumbs and blueberries and drag a skewer or wooden cocktail stick through the mixture to create streaks.

4. Divide between 4–6 individual freezerproof dishes and freeze for at least 4 hours until firm.

BANANA AND CHIA SEED PUDDINGS

Serves 4
Preparation and cooking 20 minutes + standing 30 minutes + chilling 12 hours

Ingredients:

225 ml | 8 fl oz | 1 cup coconut milk
225 g | 8 oz | 1 cup plain yoghurt
1 pinch salt
2 tbsp honey
4 tbsp chia seeds
2 bananas
ground cinnamon

Method:

1. Whisk together the coconut milk, yoghurt, salt and honey until blended.

2. Whisk in the chia seeds and leave to stand for 30 minutes. Cover and chill overnight.

3. Spoon into serving glasses. Slice the bananas and arrange on top of the puddings. Sprinkle with ground cinnamon.

APPLE CHEESECAKE

Serves 4–6
Preparation and cooking 1 hour 40 minutes + chilling 13 hours

Ingredients:

For the filling:
500 g | 18 oz | 2¼ cups cottage cheese
500 g | 18 oz | 2 cups Greek yoghurt
2 cooking apples, peeled, cored, sliced
50 g | 1¾ oz | ¼ cup white (granulated) sugar
4 tbsp runny honey
1 large egg
1 tbsp cornflour (cornstarch)
1 tsp vanilla extract
few drops green food colouring, optional

For the pastry:
200 g | 7 oz | 1¾ cups plain (all-purpose flour)
1 pinch salt
125 g | 4½ oz | ½ cup butter
1 tbsp caster (superfine) sugar
water

To decorate:
icing (confectioner's) sugar

Method:

1. For the filling: put the cottage cheese into a food processor and blend until smooth. Stir in the yoghurt and spoon the mixture into a muslin-lined sieve set over a bowl. Cover with cling wrap (plastic film) and chill for 12 hours to drain off the excess liquid.

2. For the pastry: mix the flour and salt in a mixing bowl and rub in the butter until the mixture resembles breadcrumbs. Stir in the sugar. Gradually add just enough water to form a dough. If the dough is crumbly add more water. If it is wet and sticky, add a little more flour. Form the dough into a ball, wrap in cling wrap and chill for 1 hour.

3. Heat the oven to 160°C (140°C fan | 325°F | gas 3). Grease a 22–23 cm | 8–9" deep springform tart tin.

4. Roll out the dough on a lightly floured surface and line the base and sides of the tin.

5. Heat a large frying pan (skillet) over a medium heat. Toss the apple slices with the sugar and add to the pan. Cook for 4–5 minutes, shaking the pan occasionally to prevent the apples from burning, until the apples are tender. Place the apples on a tray to cool.

6. Tip the yoghurt mixture into a clean bowl, discarding the liquid. Beat in the honey, egg, cornflour (cornstarch) and vanilla. Beat in the colouring if using.

7. Arrange the apples on the pastry base. Pour in the filling.

8. Bake for about 45 minutes until the edges are set but the centre is still slightly wobbly. Cool completely in the oven, then remove and place on a serving plate. Sift over a little icing (confectioner's) sugar just before serving.

BEETROOT AND APPLE CAKE WITH ROSEWATER ICING

Makes 1 cake
Preparation and cooking 1 hour 50 minutes

Ingredients:

50 g | 1¾ oz | ¼ cup butter, melted
100 ml | 3½ fl oz | 7 tbsp sunflower oil
2 eggs
200 g | 7 oz | 1 cup (scant) light brown sugar
200 g | 7 oz | 1¾ cups self-raising flour
1 tsp baking powder
300 g | 11 oz beetroot (beets), grated
1 apple, peeled and diced
75 g | 2½ oz | ½ cup chopped walnuts
1 unwaxed orange, finely grated zest

For the filling and coating:
180 g | 6 oz | ¾ cup unsalted butter
150 g | 5 oz | 1½ cups icing (confectioner's) sugar
450 g | 16 oz | 2 cups cream cheese
1 tsp rosewater
few drops pink food colouring

To decorate:
mint leaves

Method:

1. Heat the oven to 180°C (160°C fan | 350°F | gas 4). Grease a deep 20 cm | 8" cake tin and line the base with non-stick baking paper.

2. Whisk together the butter and oil and set aside.

3. Whisk the eggs and sugar in a mixing bowl until thick. Gradually pour in the oil and butter mixture and beat well.

4. Sift in the flour and baking powder and gently stir in until blended.

5. Add the remaining ingredients and spoon into the tin.

6. Bake for 40–60 minutes until cooked through. Cool in the tin for 10 minutes, then place on a wire rack to cool completely.

7. For the filling and coating: beat the butter until very soft. Sift in the icing (confectioner's) sugar and beat well.

8. Gradually beat in the cream cheese until blended. Beat in the rosewater and food colouring.

9. Split the cake in half horizontally through the middle. Spread about one-quarter of the filling on one cake half and place the other cake half on top.

10. Spread the remaining mixture over the top and sides of the cake.

11. Decorate with mint leaves and serve.

CREAMY BERRY ICE BLOCKS

Serves 6–8
Preparation and cooking 30 minutes + chilling 1 hour + freezing 6 hours

Ingredients:

175 g | 6 oz | ¾ cup caster (superfine) sugar
150 ml | 5 fl oz | ⅔ cup water
350 g | 12 oz | 3 cups raspberries
500 g | 18 oz | 2 cups plain yoghurt
150 g | 5 oz | 1½ cups blueberries

Method:

1. Heat the sugar and water in a pan until the sugar has dissolved, bring to a boil, then pour into a jug to cool.

2. Blend the raspberries in a blender or food processor to a puree. Alternatively, mash with a potato masher.

3. Push the puree into a sieve and push into a bowl, using the back of a spoon.

4. Stir in the sugar syrup and chill for at least 1 hour.

5. Whisk the yoghurt into the puree.

6. Churn in an ice-cream machine according to the manufacturer's instructions.

7. Alternatively, pour into a freezerproof container and freeze for 4 hours, beating with a fork 2–3 times to break up the ice crystals.

8. Crush the blueberries and add to the partially frozen mixture. Mix lightly.

9. Spoon into ice block moulds and freeze for 1 hour until firm.

10. Remove the moulds from the freezer and place a stick in the centre of each mould. Return the moulds to the freezer for 2 hours, until completely frozen and firm.

BEETROOT MUFFINS

Makes 9 muffins
Preparation and cooking 1 hour

Ingredients:

175 g | 6 oz cooked beetroot (beets)
175 g | 6 oz | ¾ cup caster (superfine) sugar
175 g | 6 oz | ¾ cup unsalted butter
3 large eggs, separated
175 g | 6 oz | 1½ cups self-raising flour
few drops vanilla extract
3 tsp poppy seeds

Method:

1. Heat the oven to 180°C (160°C fan | 350°F | gas 4). Place paper cases in 9 muffin tins.

2. Put the beetroot (beets) into a food processor or blender and blend to a puree. Set aside.

3. Beat the sugar and butter in a mixing bowl until light and creamy. Add the egg yolks, flour, pureed beetroot and vanilla and beat until smooth.

4. In a clean bowl, whisk the egg whites until stiff but not dry. Beat a large spoonful of egg white into the beetroot mixture until blended, then gradually fold in the remaining egg whites until incorporated. Stir in the poppy seeds.

5. Spoon into the paper cases and bake for about 20 minutes until risen and springy to the touch. Cool in the tins for 5 minutes and then place on a wire rack to cool completely.

DRINKS

These drink recipes include a refreshing Blueberry Mint Tea, an indulgent Eggnog and a range of colourful smoothies. Enjoy these blends of fresh ingredients and drink your way to good health.

YOGHURT SMOOTHIES

Serves 1–2
Preparation and cooking 10 minutes

Ingredients:

Basic recipe:
225 ml | 8 fl oz | 1 cup milk
1 banana, cut into chunks
175 g | 6 oz | ¾ cup plain yoghurt
honey, optional
125 ml | 4 fl oz | ½ cup of chosen fruit

Fruit choices:
peaches (orange drink), bananas (yellow drink), strawberries (pink drink), blackcurrant (purple drink), avocado (green drink)

Method:

1. Peel the fruit of choice, if appropriate, and cut into small pieces.

2. Put all the ingredients into a blender or food processor and puree until smooth. Sweeten to taste with honey if desired.

3. Pour into chilled glasses.

APPLE AND GINGER SMOOTHIES

Serves 4
Preparation and cooking 15 minutes

Ingredients:

4 apples, cored and coarsely chopped
4 cm | 1½" piece ginger (gingerroot), sliced
6 sprigs mint, leaves
½ cucumber, coarsely chopped
2–3 tbsp lime juice
water, if needed

To garnish:
chopped sunflower seeds

Method:

1. Put all the ingredients into a blender or food processor and blend until smooth.

2. If it is too thick, add a small amount of water and blend again.

3. Chill before pouring into chilled glasses. Sprinkle with sunflower seeds.

BLUEBERRY MINT TEA

Serves 4
Preparation and cooking 20 minutes

Ingredients:

150 g | 5 oz | 1½ cups blueberries
100 ml | 3½ fl oz | 7 tbsp water
8–10 mint leaves
330 ml | 12 fl oz | 1⅓ cups boiling water
honey

To garnish:
mint
edible flowers

Method:

1. Put the blueberries and water in a pan and bring to a boil, pressing the blueberries to release their juices. Stir and simmer gently for about 5 minutes.

2. Pour the blueberry juice through a sieve into a bowl.

3. Lightly bruise the mint leaves and sprinkle into the boiling water. Cover and leave to stand for 5 minutes. Pour through a fine sieve to remove the mint leaves.

4. Mix the blueberry juice with the mint-infused boiling water. Add honey to taste.

5. Serve hot or chilled with ice.

6. Garnish with mint and edible flowers.

EGGNOG

Serves 6
Preparation and cooking 20 minutes

Ingredients:

450 ml | 16 fl oz | 2 cups milk
1 tsp vanilla extract
3 cloves
½ tsp ground cinnamon
4 egg yolks
550 g | 19 oz | 2⅓ cups plain Greek yoghurt

To serve:
grated nutmeg
6 cinnamon sticks

Method:

1. Heat the milk, vanilla, cloves and cinnamon in a pan and bring to a simmer. Cook gently for 10 minutes. Remove from the heat and set aside.

2. Whisk the egg yolks, then whisk into the warm milk mixture. Leave to stand until cool.

3. Pour through a sieve into a jug and add the yoghurt. Mix well.

4. Pour into serving cups and sprinkle with grated nutmeg. Place a cinnamon stick in each cup.

CUCUMBER AND AVOCADO SMOOTHIES

Serves 4
Preparation and cooking 10 minutes

Ingredients:

1 cucumber, peeled, seeds removed and roughly chopped
1 avocado, peeled and stone removed
500 g | 18 oz | 2 cups plain yoghurt
4 kiwi fruit, peeled and roughly chopped

Method:

1. Place all the ingredients in a blender and blend until smooth.

2. Pour into glasses and serve immediately.

BLUEBERRY YOGHURT SMOOTHIES

Serves 4
Preparation and cooking 15 minutes

Ingredients:

150 g | 5 oz | ⅔ cup plain yoghurt
2 ripe bananas
300 g | 11 oz | 3 cups blueberries
few drops vanilla extract
300 ml | 11 fl oz | 1⅓ cups milk

Method:

1. Put all the ingredients in a food processor or blender and blend until smooth.

2. Pour into chilled glasses. Serve immediately.

RASPBERRY AND BEETROOT SMOOTHIES

Serves 4
Preparation and cooking 15 minutes

Ingredients:

150 g | 5 oz cooked beetroot (beets), coarsely chopped
120 g | 4 oz | 1 cup raspberries
250 ml | 9 fl oz | 1 cup cranberry juice, chilled
200 g | 7 oz | ⅞ cup plain yoghurt
lime juice

Method:

1. Puree the beetroot (beets), raspberries and cranberry juice in a blender or food processor until smooth.

2. Pour through a sieve into a large jug. Whisk in the yoghurt.

3. Add a little lime juice to taste.

4. Pour into chilled glasses and serve immediately.

GREEN SUPERFOOD SMOOTHIES

Serves 4
Preparation and cooking 15 minutes

Ingredients:

4 apples, coarsely chopped
2 sticks celery, chopped
1 zucchini (courgette), chopped
⅓ cucumber, chopped
large handful spinach
large handful watercress
2 avocados, peeled and halved
lemon juice, to taste
crushed ice

To garnish:
celery leaves

Method:

1. Put all the ingredients except the ice in a food processor or blender and blend until smooth.

2. Add crushed ice and blend again. If it is too thick, add more ice.

3. Pour into chilled glasses and serve immediately garnished with celery leaves.

WEIGHTS AND MEASURES

Weights and measures differ from country to country, but with these handy conversion charts cooking has never been easier!

Cup Measurements

One cup of these commonly used ingredients is equal to the following weights.

Ingredient	Metric	Imperial
Apples (dried and chopped)	125 g	4½ oz
Apricots (dried and chopped)	190 g	6¾ oz
Breadcrumbs (packet)	125 g	4½ oz
Breadcrumbs (soft)	55 g	2 oz
Butter	225 g	8 oz
Cheese (shredded/grated)	115 g	4 oz
Choc bits	155 g	5½ oz
Coconut (desiccated/fine)	90 g	3 oz
Flour (plain/all-purpose, self-raising)	115 g	4 oz
Fruit (dried)	170 g	6 oz
Golden syrup (golden corn syrup)	315 g	11 oz
Honey	315 g	11 oz
Margarine	225 g	8 oz
Nuts (chopped)	115 g	4 oz
Rice (cooked)	155 g	5½ oz
Rice (uncooked)	225 g	8 oz
Sugar (brown)	155 g	5½ oz
Sugar (caster/superfine)	225 g	8 oz
Sugar (white/ granulated)	225 g	8 oz
Sugar (sifted, icing/confectioner's)	155 g	5½ oz
Treacle (molasses)	315 g	11 oz

Oven Temperatures

Celsius	Fahrenheit	Gas mark
120	250	1
150	300	2
160	320	3
180	350	4
190	375	5
200	400	6
220	430	7
230	450	8
250	480	9

Liquid Measures

Cup	Metric	Imperial
¼ cup	63 ml	2¼ fl oz
½ cup	125 ml	4½ fl oz
¾ cup	188 ml	6⅔ fl oz
1 cup	250 ml	8¾ fl oz
1¾ cup	438 ml	15½ fl oz
2 cups	500 ml	17½ fl oz
4 cups	1 litre	35 fl oz

Spoon	Metric	Imperial
¼ teaspoon	1.25 ml	⅟₂₅ fl oz
½ teaspoon	2.5 ml	⅟₁₂ fl oz
1 teaspoon	5 ml	⅙ fl oz
1 tablespoon	15 ml	½ fl oz

Weight Measures

Metric	Imperial
10 g	¼ oz
15 g	½ oz
20 g	¾ oz
30 g	1 oz
60 g	2 oz
115 g	4 oz (¼ lb)
125 g	4½ oz
145 g	5 oz
170 g	6 oz
185 g	6½ oz
200 g	7 oz
225 g	8 oz (½ lb)
300 g	10½ oz
330 g	11½ oz
370 g	13 oz
400 g	14 oz
425 g	15 oz
455 g	16 oz (1 lb)
500 g	17½ oz (1 lb 1½ oz)
600 g	21 oz (1 lb 5 oz)
650 g	23 oz (1 lb 7 oz)
750 g	26½ oz (1 lb 10½ oz)
1000 g (1 kg)	35 oz (2 lb 3 oz)

INDEX